10.95

Piano • Vocal • Guitar

COMEDY SONGS
from Broadway Musicals

W9-DJL-095

INTRODUCTION

Not too many years ago the generic term for a musical was musical comedy in obvious recognition that humor was just as important to a Broadway song-and-dance show as its other ingredients. Even today, when some of the sellout attractions seem more anxious to make us weep than to laugh, there is always at least one comic number to remind us that a Broadway musical is not an opera.

This collection offers 17 such songs. They might be written to reveal character ("Adelaide's Lament" and "Kids") or they might even have something to do with the stories being told ("Little Tin Box" and "Mutual Admiration Society"). Most of them, however, were simply included in a score for no other reason than to provoke audience merriment while still, somehow, fitting into the overall mood and action of the production. Often these numbers and the way they were performed are recalled by theatregoers more clearly than many of the other songs in a show. And though few have ever become pop hits, they were the pieces that, on occasion, even required their creators to write additional verses as audiences clamored for encore after encore. They were the show stoppers.

Stanley Green
Author of BROADWAY
MUSICALS - SHOW BY SHOW

CONTENTS

ISBN 0-88188-857-5

HAL•LEONARD®
CORPORATION
7777 W. BLUEMOUND RD. P.O. BOX 13819 MILWAUKEE, WI 53213

ABOUT THE SONGS...

ADELAIDE'S LAMENT
The jeremaid of a frustrated woman who suffers from a psychosomatic cold resulting from the continuing postponement of her marriage may hardly seem to be the material for a musical number, comic or otherwise, but composer-lyricist Frank Loesser managed to make it not only musical and comical but even a bit poignant. Written before the book of **Guys and Dolls** had reached even the talking stage, the song establishes the character of Miss Adelaide, the featured attraction at the Hot Box nightclub and one of the principal inhabitants of the flashy Broadway world that was first brought to life in the short stories of Damon Runyon. Vivian Blaine, who introduced the number in the original 1950 production, repeated her role in the film version five years later.

BRUSH UP YOUR SHAKESPEARE
Since **Kiss Me, Kate,** the 1948 Cole Porter hit, dealt with a production of a musical version of Shakespeare's **The Taming of the Shrew,** one of the composer's bright ideas was to include a number, "Brush Up Your Shakespeare," sung by two stage-struck hoods (originally played by Harry Clark and Jack Diamond) that paid homage to no less than 14 of the Bard's 36 plays, while offering the novel advice that quoting from them could serve as a literary aphrodisiac. The stars of **Kiss Me, Kate** were Alfred Drake and Patricia Morison who played characters whose offstage battles were at least equal to their onstage confrontations.

CIVILIZATION (BONGO, BONGO, BONGO)
In Carl Sigman and Bob Hilliard's bright Calypso number, a proud African native happily resists the blandishments of what passes for civilization with its "bright lights, false teeth, door bells, and landlords." One of the rare Broadway comic songs to become a pop hit, "Civilization (Bongo, Bongo, Bongo)" was officially introduced by an excessively energetic Elaine Stritch making her Broadway debut in the 1947 intimate revue, **Angel in the Wings.** The "officially" is used because not only did the song become popular (its recording by Danny Kaye and the Andrews Sisters was a best seller), it was being played and sung even before the show opened.

EADIE WAS A LADY
Written by Richard A. Whiting and B.G. DeSylva, "Eadie Was a Lady" was performed in the 1932 backstage musical, **Take a Chance,** as part of a show within a show. The scene is a New Orleans levee saloon at the time of the Spanish-American War, and the show-stopping number was introduced by Ethel Merman making her third appearance on Broadway. As Miss Merman recalled, "The audience was with me from the moment I came downstairs swinging my hips in my American Beauty red satin dress and a black boa around my shoulders. As I launched into this serio-comic paean to my dead sister in sin, I felt the current that runs back and forth when something extraordinary is happening onstage. Hearing about this shady lady, who was so refined she drank her brandy with her pinkie sticking out, the audience was convulsed by her 'savior-fairy' and, as the song said, her 'class with a capital K.' "

'ERBIE FITCH'S TWITCH
The tale of a philandering bloke from Ipswitch was one of the applause-catching numbers in **Redhead,** a Broadway success of the 1958/59 season. In the words of **Variety's** critic, Hobe Morrison, "In this spectacularly entertaining music hall-style song, composer Albert Hague and lyricist Dorothy Fields have created a number that's a cinch for the memory books of musical-comedy buffs." The murder mystery musical, set in and around a wax museum in turn-of-the-century London, starred Gwen Verdon who introduced the patter song wearing a bowler hat and baggy pants in imitation of the way her daddy performed the number in his music-hall act.

EVERYBODY OUGHT TO HAVE A MAID
Just about the only production with songs by Stephen Sondheim that could be termed a musical comedy – even a musical farce – was **A Funny Thing Happened on the Way to the Forum,** which opened on Broadway in 1962. With broadly written characters based on those created by ancient Rome's most celebrated comic playwright, Titus Maccius Plautus (254 BC-184 BC), the complicated slam-bang plot at one point is concerned with a self-described lovely – and virginal – courtesan who has just been made a new member of the household staff of a lecherous slaveowner. And that's the cue for a riotous four-part tribute extolling the virtues of maids, particularly ones that are "obedient and pliable." Singing the praises in the original cast were David Burns (as the slaveowner), Zero Mostel and Jack Gilford (as two of his slaves), and John Carradine (as the local dealer in courtesans).

HONEY BUN
Richard Rodgers and Oscar Hammerstein's tale of World War II, **South Pacific,** tells a generally serious story of the romance between a Navy nurse and a French planter on a Pacific island and the way that romance is almost destroyed by racial prejudice. In the second act, however, there is one number in a Thanksgiving Day show put on by nurses and Seabees that has nothing more on its mind than to bring down the house – which it never fails to do. Introduced in the original 1949 production by Mary Martin in a sailor uniform at least three sizes too big, the sprightly piece describes the sailor's inamorata – known as Honey Bun – who is as dainty as a sparrow, weighs a hundred and one pounds, and stands sixty inches high. After the second refrain, the singer is joined in a dance by one of the Seabees outlandishly dressed as a South Sea Siren. Among the longest running shows in Broadway history, **South Pacific** was awarded the Pulitzer Prize for drama.

JUBILATION T. CORNPONE
Johnny Mercer's rare affinity for regional comic lyrics and Gene de Paul's lively tunes were perfectly suited to the 1956 musical version of the comic strip **Li'l Abner.** A satire on militarism, venal politicians, and conformity, the show looked at the world through the eyes of the denizens of Dogpatch, USA, among whom are Moonbeam McSwine, Marryin' Sam, General Bullmoose, and Appassionata Von Climax. Marryin Sam (originally played by Stubby Kaye) is the one who gets the chance to sing the show's big number, "Jubilation T. Cornpone," a rousing panagyric extolling the accomplishments of the Confederacy's most incompetent general.

KIDS
The first Broadway musical to deal with the phenomenom of rock and roll and its influence on teenagers, **Bye Bye Birdie** takes a satirical but affectionate view of the youngsters of Sweet Apple, Ohio, who get a chance to meet an Elvis Presley-type singing idol when he visits their town before being drafted. Starring Dick Van Dyke and Chita Rivera, the show benefited from the clever parodying of the rock sound of 1960 created by composer Charles Strouse and lyricist Lee Adams, here writing their first Broadway score. Among the highlights is the sight of the fatuous father of one of the teenage girls (Paul Lynde did the part originally) blowing off steam at the manners and mores of kids today, and plaintively asking, "Why can't they be like we were, perfect in every way?"

LE GRAND BOOM BOOM

Like most other songs in Broadway musicals, "Le Grand Boom Boom" had nothing whatever to do with the plot of **Little Me** but was inserted in the 1962 musical as a specialty number for the star, Sid Caesar, who played no less than seven different roles in the show. In Caesar's first appearance as Val du Val, an exuberant French entertainer, he introduces the number by explaining that he will sing a song of love, "not the little love that goes plinky linky plink, but the French love that goes BOOM-BOOM." Cy Coleman and Carolyn Leigh wrote the musical's witty score and Neil Simon provided the outlandish plot all about well-proportioned Belle Poitrine whose numerous adventures take her from Drifter's Row, Venezuela, Illinois, all the way to a Southampton estate and a final fadeout with the one man she has always loved.

LIFE UPON THE WICKED STAGE

Jerome Kern and Oscar Hammerstein's trailblazing musical, **Show Boat,** which opened on Broadway in 1927, is the oldest show represented in this collection. Its by-now familiar story, based on Edna Ferber's novel, concerns the fortunes of Magnolia Hawks, whose father runs the showboat Cotton Blossom, and her ill-starred romance with the dashing riverboat gambler Gaylord Ravenal. While **Show Boat** may have been a notable departure from the frivolous musical comedies of the twenties, the author did manage to find room for the perky comic number, "Life Upon the Wicked Stage," in which showboat trouper Ellie Mae Chipley (originally played by Eva Puck) tells a bevy of starry-eyed young ladies all about her disillusionment with the terribly tame life that she leads.

LITTLE TIN BOX

Toward the end of Act II of the 1959 Pulitzer Prize-winning musical, **Fiorello!,** a New York politician (originally Howard Da Silva) and his fellow Republican ward heelers are discussing the latest scandals to come out of the Seabury Investigation of city corruption under Democratic Mayor Jimmy Walker. As they gleefully recreate the hearings (which would help bring Mayor Fiorello La Guardia to power), they offer the testimony of three city officials who cynically explain in tones of shocked innocence how, from meager salaries, they have managed to put away enough pennies into a Little Tin Box to afford a yacht, a Rolls Royce, and the pleasures of a dozen women in fancy hotels. Written by Jerry Bock and Sheldon Harnick, the number never failed to stop the show at every performance.

MUTUAL ADMIRATION SOCIETY

An Ethel Merman musical was always a major theatrical event, even though **Happy Hunting,** in 1956, was never in quite the same league as most of her other shows. Taking its inspiration from the headlines, the plot was about a society-crashing rich Philadelphian who has traveled with her daughter all the way to Monaco, only to be denied an invitation to the Grace Kelly-Prince Rainier nuptials. To help buck up their spirits – and to show how they feel about each other – mother and daughter exchange compliments in the bouncy "Mutual Admiration Society," far and away the most popular number in the Harold Karr-Matt Dubey score.

THE TALE OF THE OYSTER

Possibly the only song ever written about regurgitation, "The Tale of the Oyster" was one of the sparkling numbers that Cole Porter wrote for the 1929 "Musical Comedy Tour of Paris" called **Fifty Million Frenchmen.** Though this saga of the social climbing marine mollusk has enjoyed a certain amount of popularity in recent years (it was even sung on a televised tribute to Porter from the White House in 1987), when Helen Broderick introduced it in the show audiences were not amused and the song was dropped during the run. (It had nothing to do with the story, anyway.) Actually, "The Tale of the Oyster" was a reworking of an earlier Cole Porter piece called "The Scampi," written to amuse the affluent and titled pre-jet set crowd on the Lido.

TO KEEP MY LOVE ALIVE

In 1943, when composer Richard Rodgers decided to revive his biggest hit of the twenties, **A Connecticut Yankee,** he and lyricist Lorenz Hart also decided to drop five songs in the original score and replace them with six new numbers. One of them, "To Keep My Love Alive," turned out to be among the cleverest show-stoppers the team ever wrote. A comic threnody in the form of a dainty madrigal, it was originally sung in the show by Vivienne Segal as the much-married Queen Morgan Le Fay who calmly itemizes the various ways in which she has managed to bump off everyone of her spouses – from removing an appendix to poisoning, stabbing, choking, and beheading. In the story, based on the Mark Twain novel, the title character dreams that he is back in the days of King Arthur's Camelot where he becomes a court favorite by introducing modern technology and assembly-line efficiency.

TRIPLETS

Though the frisky diatribe "Triplets" was immortalized by Fred Astaire, Nanette Fabray, and Jack Buchanan as they scampered about on their knees in baby clothes in the film **The Band Wagon,** the number dates back to 1937 when it was sung by the Tune Twisters in a cabaret scene in **Between the Devil,** a Broadway musical also starring Mr. Buchanan. The show may have boasted some of Arthur Schwartz and Howard Dietz's most captivating novelty items and ballads (such as "By Myself" and "I See Your Face Before Me"), but the tale of a bigamist with both an English wife and a French wife somehow never caught on with the public and the musical ended its run after only three months.

TSCHAIKOWSKY

Back in 1924, Ira Gershwin had written a piece of light verse, "The Music Hour," which was published in Life magazine and in which he had managed to include the names of 49 Russian composers, both living and dead. Seventeen years later, when a number was needed for Danny Kaye in the Circus Dream Sequence in **Lady in the Dark,** Gershwin remembered the poem and he and composer Kurt Weill simply used it as the lyric for a virtuoso patter song, which they dubbed "Tschaikowsky." Since rapid-fire, tongue-twisting numbers were a Danny Kaye specialty, the comedian was able to rip through the songs in 39 seconds flat. The musical, which starred Gertrude Lawrence and was concerned with the effects of psychiatry on a modern career woman, reserved all the songs but one ("My Ship") for the three dream sequences designed to show us how the heroine got to be the way she was.

ADELAIDE'S LAMENT
(From "GUYS AND DOLLS")

By FRANK LOESSER

Edited by Wm. Ellfeldt

Symbols for Guitar, Diagrams for Ukulele.

fect-ing the up-per res-pir-a-tor-y tract. *(Adelaide reacts)* In
volv-ing the eye, the ear and the nose and throat. *(Adelaide reacts)* In

oth-er words, just from wait-ing a-round for that plain lit-tle band of gold, A
oth-er words, just from wor-ry-ing wheth-er the wed-ding is on or off, A

per-son_____ can de-vel-op a cold. You can
per-son_____ can de-vel-op a cough. You can

spray her wher-ev-er you fig-ure the strep-to-coc-ci lurk,— You can
feed her all day with the Vi-ta-min A and the Bro-mo Fizz,— But the

BRUSH UP YOUR SHAKESPEARE
(From "KISS ME KATE")

Words and Music by
COLE PORTER

The girls to-day in so-ci-e-ty Go for class-i-cal po-et-ry, So, to win their hearts, one must quote with ease Aes-chy-lus and Eu-ri-pi-

des, One must know Hom-er and b'lieve me, bo, Soph - o - cles,

al - so Sap - pho - ho, Un - less you know Shel - ley and Keats and

Pope, Dain - ty deb-bies will call you a dope. But the po - et

of them all _____ Who will start 'em sim - ply

sfz

13

CIVILIZATION
(BONGO, BONGO, BONGO)
(From "ANGEL IN THE WINGS")

Words and Music by BOB HILLIARD
and CARL SIGMAN

Moderately

'ERBIE FITCH'S TWITCH

Words and Music by DOROTHY FIELDS
and ALBERT HAGUE

switch to the witch which gives you a twitch, which witch is not rich as the witch you wed in-

stead. Crawl in-to your niche And take Mis - sus Fitch to

bed.

Dance

EADIE WAS A LADY

Words and Music by RICHARD WHITING,
NACIO HERB BROWN, B.G. DE SYLVA

Af - ter meals she'd flash it a - bout.__
Pick - ed the ones that sel - dom paid.__

'Mem - ber how she used to drink her bran - dy?
But you'd nev - er catch her with her legs crossed,

With her fin - gers stick - in' well out.__
In the wag - on af - ter the raid.__

Ea - die was a la - dy__ *All:* Ea - die was a la - dy.

EVERYBODY OUGHT TO HAVE A MAID

(From "A FUNNY THING HAPPENED ON THE WAY TO THE FORUM")

Words and Music by
STEPHEN SONDHEIM

Moderato commodo

Refrain

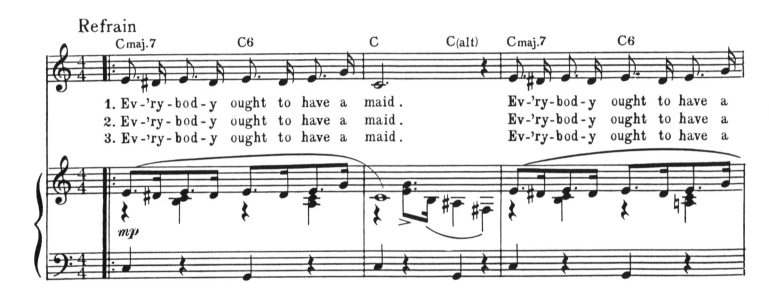

1. Ev-'ry-bod-y ought to have a maid. Ev-'ry-bod-y ought to have a
2. Ev-'ry-bod-y ought to have a maid. Ev-'ry-bod-y ought to have a
3. Ev-'ry-bod-y ought to have a maid. Ev-'ry-bod-y ought to have a

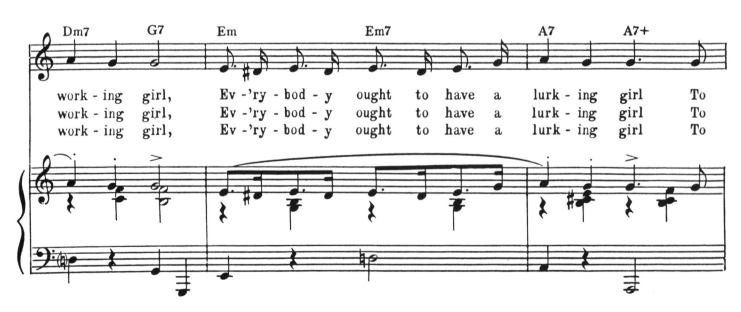

work-ing girl, Ev-'ry-bod-y ought to have a lurk-ing girl To
work-ing girl, Ev-'ry-bod-y ought to have a lurk-ing girl To
work-ing girl, Ev-'ry-bod-y ought to have a lurk-ing girl To

HONEY BUN
(From "SOUTH PACIFIC")

Words by OSCAR HAMMERSTEIN II
Music by RICHARD RODGERS

JUBILATION T. CORNPONE

Swing tempo

Words and Music by GENE DE PAUL
and JOHNNY MERCER

When we fought the Yank - ees and an -
When we al - most had 'em but the
With our am - mu - ni - tion gone and

ni - hi - la - tion was near,
is - sue still___ was in doubt,
faced with ut - ter de - feat,

Who was there to
Who sug - gest - ed
Who was it that

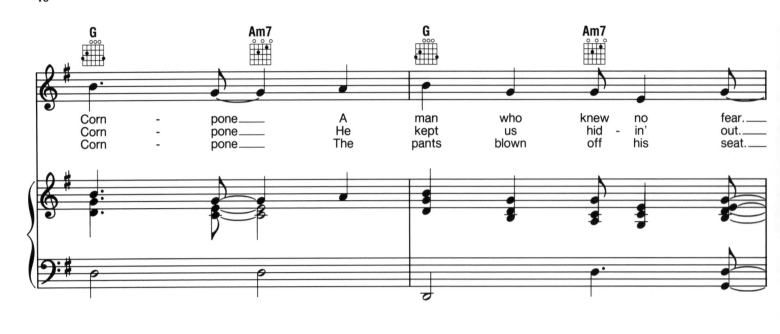

Corn - pone_____ A man who knew no fear._____
Corn - pone_____ He kept us hid - in' out._____
Corn - pone_____ The pants blown off his seat._____

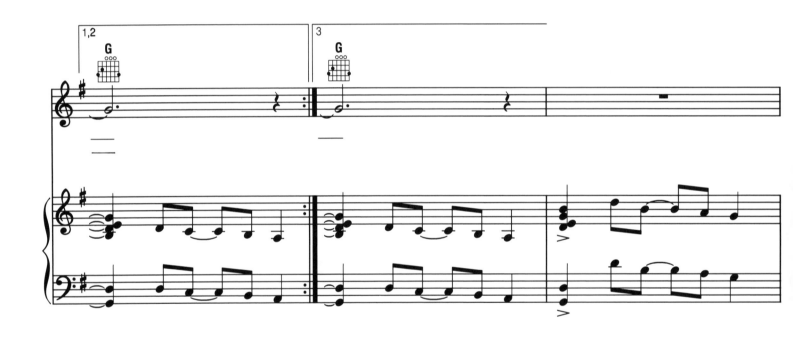

MUTUAL ADMIRATION SOCIETY
(From "HAPPY HUNTING")

Words by MATT DUBEY
Music by HAROLD KARR

Lyrics:

We be-long to a Mu-tu-al Ad-mi-ra-tion So-ci-e-ty, My ba-by and me.

We be-long to a Mu-tu-al _____

KIDS!
(From "BYE BYE BIRDIE")

Words by LEE ADAMS
Music by CHARLES STROUSE

LE GRAND BOOM BOOM

(From "Little Me")

Words by CAROLYN LEIGH
Music by CY COLEMAN

point was al-ways drowned out by the vi'-lent can-non-nad-ing of his
on the vo-cal start-er, And the rest be-comes the pound-ing of his

heart._____ He'd say, "Pier - rette!"_____ And clear his
head._____ She'll say, "Pier - rot?"_____ He'll start to

throat,_____ "Lest you for - get!"_____ And here I quote:
snore,_____ The rest you know,_____ She'll say once more: *(to 3rd Refrain)*

Refrain-Moderately bright

1. If ze girl, Boom Boom and ze boy, Boom Boom and zey
(2. If ze) man, Boom Boom and ze wife, Boom Boom 'though it's
3. If ze girl, Boom Boom and ze boy, Boom Boom and zey

mp-mf
a tempo

LIFE UPON THE WICKED STAGE

Words by OSCAR HAMMERSTEIN II
Music by JEROME KERN

LITTLE TIN BOX

Words and Music by JERRY BOCK
and SHELDON HARNICK

58

Lyrics For LITTLE TIN BOX

FOURTH HACK
Mr. "X," may we ask you a question?
It's amazing is it not?
That the city pays you slightly less
Than fifty bucks a week
Yet you've purchased a private yacht!

BEN
I am positive Your Honor must be joking
Any working man can do what I have done
For a month or two I simply gave up smoking
And I put my extra pennies one by one

Into a little tin box
A little tin box
That a little tin key unlocks
There is nothing unorthodox
About a little tin box

MEN
About a little tin box
About a little tin box

In a little tin box
A little tin box
That a little tin key unlocks

BEN
There is honor and purity

ALL
Lots of security
In a little tin box

FIFTH HACK (Speaking) Next witness.

FIRST HACK
Mr. "Y," we've been told You don't feel well
And we know you've lost your voice
But we wonder how you managed on the salary you make
To acquire a new Rolls Royce

BEN
You're implying I'm a crook and I say no sir!
There is nothing in my past I care to hide
I've been taking empty bottles to the grocer
And each nickel that I got was put aside

MEN
That he got was put aside

BEN
Into a little tin box
A little tin box
That a little tin key unlocks
There is nothing unorthodox
About a little tin box

MEN
About a little tin box
About a little tin box
In a little tin box
A little tin box
There's a cushion for life's rude shocks

BEN
There is faith, hope and charity

ALL
Hard-won prosperity
In a little tin box.

FIFTH HACK (Speaking) Next witness! Take the stand!

SIXTH HACK
Mr. "Z," you're a junior official
And your income's rather low
Yet you've kept a dozen women
In the very best hotels
Would you kindly explain, how so?

BEN
I can see Your Honor doesn't pull his punches
And it looks a trifle fishy, I'll admit
But for one whole week I went without my lunches
And it mounted up, Your Honor, bit by bit

MEN
Up Your Honor, bit by bit.
It's just a little tin box
A little tin box
That a little tin key unlocks
There is nothing unorthodox
About a little tin box
About a little tin box
In a little tin box
A little tin box
All a-glitter with blue chip stocks

BEN
There is something delectable

ALL
Almost respectable
In a little tin box
In a little tin box!

THE TALE OF THE OYSTER

Words and Music by
COLE PORTER

63

TO KEEP MY LOVE ALIVE

Words by LORENZ HART
Music by RICHARD RODGERS

Phil-ip played the harp, I cussed the thing. I crowned him with his harp to
Ath-el-stane in-dulged in frat-ri-cide, he killed his dad and that was

bust the thing, and now he plays where harps are just the thing, to
pat-ri-cide. One night I stabbed him by my mat-tress side, to

keep my love a - live, to keep my love a - live.
keep my love a - live, to

I keep my love a - live.

TRIPLETS

Words by HOWARD DIETZ
Music by ARTHUR SCHWARTZ

74

Patter

75

TSCHAIKOWSKY
(AND OTHER RUSSIANS)

(From The Musical Production "Lady In The Dark")

Words by IRA GERSHWIN
Music by KURT WEILL

78

79

real - ly have to stop, The sub - ject has been dwelt up -

ALL   RINGMASTER   ALL

on e - nough! Stra - vin - sky, Gret - chna - ni - noff, Kvo -

RINGMASTER

schin - sky, Rach - ma - ni - noff! I real - ly have to

stop be - cause you all have un - der - gone e - nough!